A MAZE ADVENTURE

SECRETS OF THE PYRAMIDS

For my son Ashley—G.W.

The publisher and packager wish to thank Stuart Tyson Smith, Assistant Professor,
Department of Anthropology, University of California, Santa Barbara, California, and George Hart,
Staff Lecturer on the Egyptian Collection at the British Museum, for their expert assistance in reviewing
the text and art in *Secrets of the Pyramids*.

Prepared for the National Geographic Society by Firecrest Books Ltd.

The art was created by Graham White on computer with watercolor software.
Book design by Phil Jacobs
The body text of the book is set in Galliard.

Library of Congress Cataloging-in-Publication Data:
White, Graham, 1953-
Secrets of the pyramids : a maze adventure / by Graham White.
p. cm.
Includes index.
Summary: In helping a twelve-year-old boy to search for his father by
solving a maze puzzle, the reader encounters information about how and
why pyramids were constructed in ancient Egypt.
ISBN 0-7922-6938-1 (pbk.)
1. Pyramids—Egypt—Juvenile literature. 2. Maze puzzles—Juvenile literature.
[1. Pyramids—Egypt. 2. Maze puzzles.] I. Title.
DT63 .W49 2002
932.01—dc21   2002001656

One of the world's largest nonprofit scientific and educational organizations, the National Geographic Society was founded in
1888 "for the increase and diffusion of geographic knowledge." Fulfilling this mission, the Society educates and inspires
millions every day through its magazines, books, television programs, videos, maps and atlases, research grants, the National
Geographic Bee, teacher workshops, and innovative classroom materials. The Society is supported through membership dues,
charitable gifts, and income from the sale of its educational products. This support is vital to National Geographic's mission
to increase global understanding and promote conservation of our planet through exploration, research, and education.

For more information, please call
1-800-NGS-LINE (647-5463) or write to the following address:
National Geographic Society
1145 17th Street N.W.
Washington, D.C. 20036-4688
U.S.A.

Visit the Society's Web site: www.nationalgeographic.com

Printed in Belgium

A MAZE ADVENTURE

SECRETS OF THE PYRAMIDS

Graham White

NATIONAL GEOGRAPHIC

Washington, D.C.

Contents

While taking every care to check the facts presented in this book and the validity of the drawings, the publishers have allowed a certain amount of "artistic license" to enable the artist to create the mazes and tell a story. This has involved, for example, the inclusion of staircases, ladders, and some of the tunnels and chambers, etc, to provide the routes and spaces needed for the mazes. In addition, the styles of architecture and painting throughout the book are meant to represent ancient Egypt generally, and the story and the coded puzzle are entirely fictional.

To complete the mazes, follow the clearly defined paths. You may go up and down stairs and ladders, behind pillars, etc., but no hopping over low walls or other obstructions that might look easy to climb over.

8

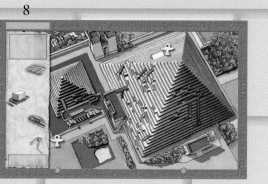

10

12

14

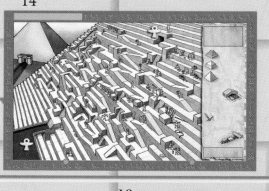

16

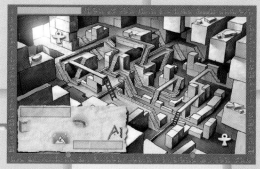

18

20

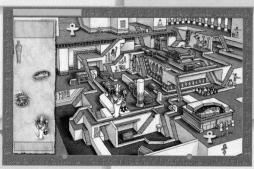

22

26

Welcome to Ancient Egypt

Welcome to the world of ancient Egypt, the land of the pyramids. These enormous tombs are the largest structures ever built. They are prepared for our pharaohs, or kings, who are buried in them when they die.

My name is Hemon. I am 12 years old and have three brothers and two sisters. We live in a small village close to where two new pyramids are being built.

The body of our Pharaoh has just been laid deep inside the larger pyramid, where he will begin his journey to the afterlife. Lots of things that he will need have been buried with him. I have helped to build his pyramid myself, and this means I will share in my Pharaoh's life after death. And so will my father, who has worked on the pyramid since long before I was born. It has taken thousands of men more than 20 years to build the pyramid, and it just needs some finishing off to make the outer slopes nice and smooth.

My family is poor and cannot afford to send me to school. So every night before I go to sleep my father tells me wonderful stories of the pyramids and teaches me all about them. If you want to know about pyramids, you've come to the right person!

But today I am very worried. My father did not return from his work as usual after sundown. I have not seen him since last night, when, during our private time together, he told me about a secret entrance into the Pharaoh's pyramid that he and a few chosen others had been sent to work on. He told me also that such workers on other pyramids have been accidentally sealed inside because few people knew they were there. I believe this has now happened to my dear father, and I am determined to find the secret entrance and rescue him. But I must hurry. It can't be long before his work is completed and he is trapped for eternity.

Will you help me? You will? Good! I will teach you everything my father has told me about the pyramids, and on our journey together we will uncover many more secrets within.

Let us prepare. We'll start by having a look at a plan of the pyramid on the next page.

Maze 1. The Plan

Before we begin our adventure, we must study my father's plan. He has marked out the main walkways used by the workers, which may help us to find the secret entrance later. Try to work your way through the maze. If you succeed, you have what it takes to travel with me in search of my father.

Before any building could begin on the pyramids, the ground had to be prepared to make it level. To do this, we dug lots of connecting trenches and then poured water into them. At the water level, lines were marked on the trench walls. We carefully chipped away all the ground above these marks. The result was a perfectly flat and level surface to build on.

Most of the stones came from a nearby quarry, but a few large granite stones were brought up the River Nile on boats, some from 600 miles away. My father was one of the many workers needed to drag them from the riverside on sledges up to the stonemasons for cutting. He worked long hours and was rewarded with food—usually vegetables. I helped lubricate the clay ramps with water.

We built mortuary temples next to the pyramids. The Pharaoh's body was brought here to be mummified— wrapped and preserved. Then, priests recited magical spells before the body was taken for burial. These spells made sure the Pharaoh would rise up toward the sun god to begin his eternal life.

All pyramids are built on the west bank of the river because, my father explained, that is the way the sun travels. To wake to a new life, the Pharaoh must travel toward the west, too.

We must hurry now. My father needs our help, and we have much to do. Our first task is to make our way through the village to the pyramids beyond. So turn the page and let's begin!

START

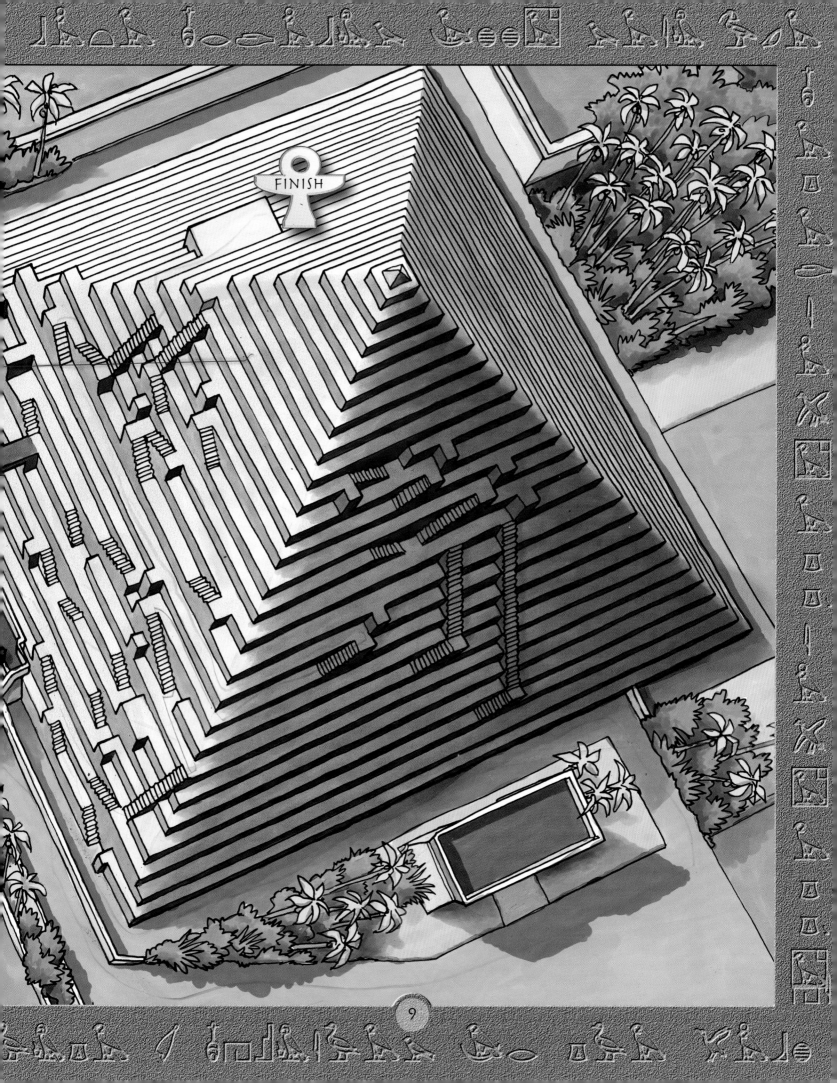

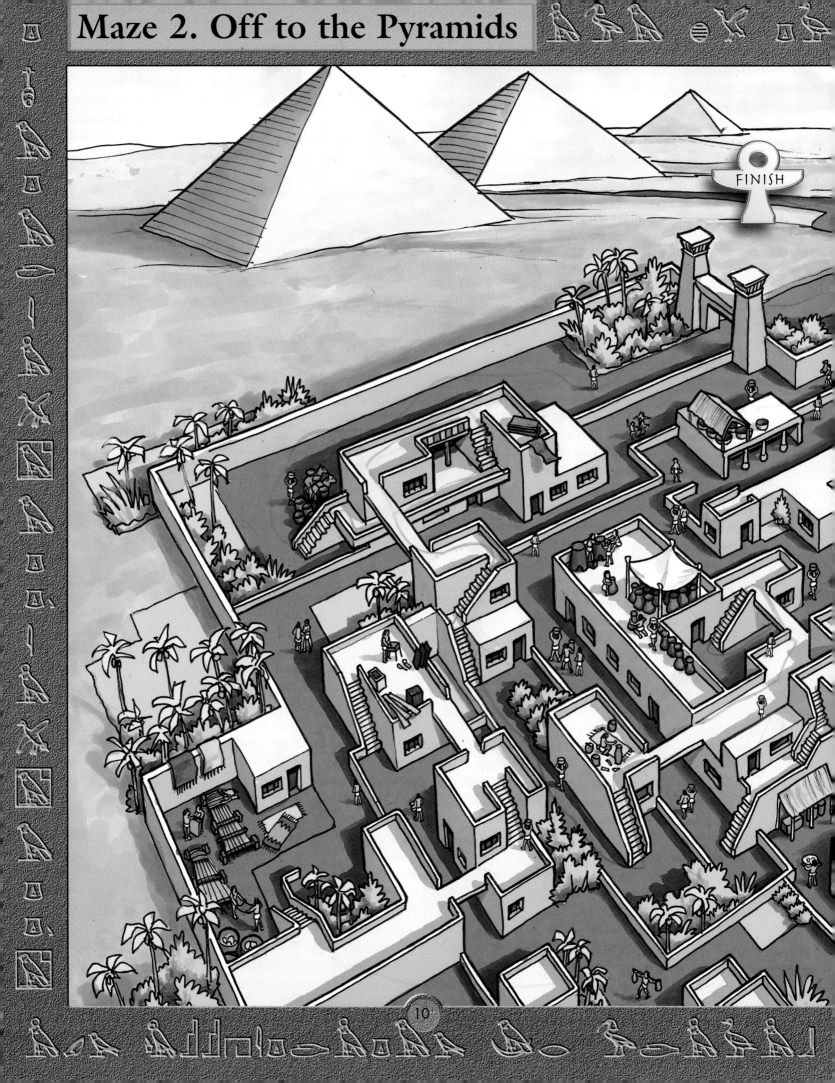

FINISH

START

Our village has been specially built here so that we live close to the pyramids. But before we can set off along the road toward them, we have to make our way through it. There are twists and turns, and people are milling around. But we mustn't take too long—father will be waiting.

My village is usually a very lively place. People make pottery, baskets, and furniture, while others weave mats and fine linen. Farmers work outside the village on rich fertile land around the River Nile. My mother bakes her own bread, which is delicious. I have a friend who makes toys, and mother says that, if I'm good and work hard, she will give him some bread in exchange for my favorite toy.

All the buildings in the village except the Temple are made from mud bricks. Two of my brothers help with brickmaking. They use mud from the riverbank, adding chopped straw and animal hair for extra strength. They place this mixture in wooden brick molds, turning them out to dry in the sun for two or three days. The buildings are then plastered over with mud to protect the bricks.

Our windows are small to keep out the hot sunlight. And, where possible, doors face north to catch the breeze, which blows from north to south. Our house is very simple. We have three rooms, with steps leading up to the flat roof where we all sit during the cooler evenings. Richer families have larger houses with more rooms.

The most important building is the Temple, the house of our gods. But it is not only a place for worship. It contains the school, workshops, and storehouses, too.

After the village, we have a short walk through the hot desert to the pyramids, so don't forget the water!

FINISH

This is the pyramid site. Many experts are involved in the building of pyramids. Architects and mathematicians calculate measurements, stonemasons shape the blocks, and overseers organize the teams of laborers. My father was working on the large pyramid to the left. We have to find our way there quickly.

The pyramid is not yet completed. There are more stones to be added. Once the core, or inner part, is finished, the whole building is faced with pure white limestone, which makes it gleam in the sun. Our highly skilled masons cut these stones so precisely that, when they are in position, you cannot push a hair between them!

Workers build ramps to move the huge blocks up the pyramid. These ramps wind around the structure as it grows. Moving the blocks is very hazardous, and many workers are killed or injured during the construction. Altogether, there are over two million blocks in the pyramid!

My oldest brother is a metalworker. He is kept busy repairing and replacing the bronze and copper blades. He also shapes wooden wedges that are driven into cracks in the stone. When soaked with water, these expand and can produce enough force to split a great stone in half.

Some stonemasons carve statues, which are placed inside the pyramid to protect the Pharaoh. The statue of a sphinx on the right is to guard the pyramid from thieves. Its human head and lion's body stand for royal power.

Be careful as you find your way through. The ground is very uneven here, and there are many sharp stones scattered around.

START

START

FINISH

At last we are at the pyramid. But it is so big! Workmen are still busy moving the last few limestone blocks into position. We must find our way through them to the secret entrance that my father spoke of. I hope you have a good head for heights!

When the pyramid is finished, it will have smooth, flat sides. The first pyramid-shaped tombs had stepped sides—like a "stairway" to the stars. Then the architects tried a smooth-sided design. But they found the angle of the sides a little too steep, so halfway up they changed to a more gentle slope. I think the smooth, straight pyramids we build today are perfect!

At the base of the pyramid is a layer of about 30,000 blocks! A burial chamber is built into its center, where our Pharaoh is laid to rest. This must have extra-strong walls to support the great weight of the pyramid above, so granite blocks are used. They are much harder and stronger than the limestone ones.

Granite is also used for sealing the entrance tunnel. A granite block is positioned in a sloping tunnel above the entrance passageway. When everything inside has been completed, the block is released, sealing the Pharaoh from the outside world for all eternity. I hope my father is not trapped for all eternity, too!

All the Pharaoh's belongings are buried with him for his use in the afterlife, even his boat. This is buried in a specially made pit next to the pyramid. The walls of the pit are plastered to make them airtight, and large stone slabs are dragged across to form the roof.

Climbing the pyramid is hard work! But don't give up. If we find the secret entrance soon, we can rest inside, where it will be much cooler.

15

START

This must be it—the secret tunnel that my father is working on. He can't be far away now. But it is going to be difficult to find a way through.

The many pyramid workers are split into more than a hundred teams. Each team strives to be the best. My father's team is called "The Lions." Teams mark some of the stones they lay with graffiti perhaps boasting that they are the quickest or most efficient. Look! Here's a mark left by my father's team. We must be on the right track!

Narrow shafts inside the pyramid line up with certain stars. Some point to Orion, some to the polar stars. Orion houses the soul of Osiris, the god of the dead, who will now give our Pharaoh a new home in the afterlife. The shafts also provide air to enable workers to breathe deep inside the pyramid.

The site of the pyramid was carefully chosen by the architects, and a ceremony was held where tools and charms were offered as gifts to the gods. For the Pharaoh's soul to fly north to the stars, one side of the pyramid must face north. True north is found by creating an angle between where a star rises and where it sets. Half this angle points exactly toward north.

The overseers make sure that every block is placed so that it is level and perfectly upright before another is put on top. Our tools for this are simple. They are the "right angle" and the "plumb level."

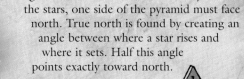

We can't rest for long—I think the entrance will be sealed soon. We must find our way through the tunnel before we are trapped for eternity!

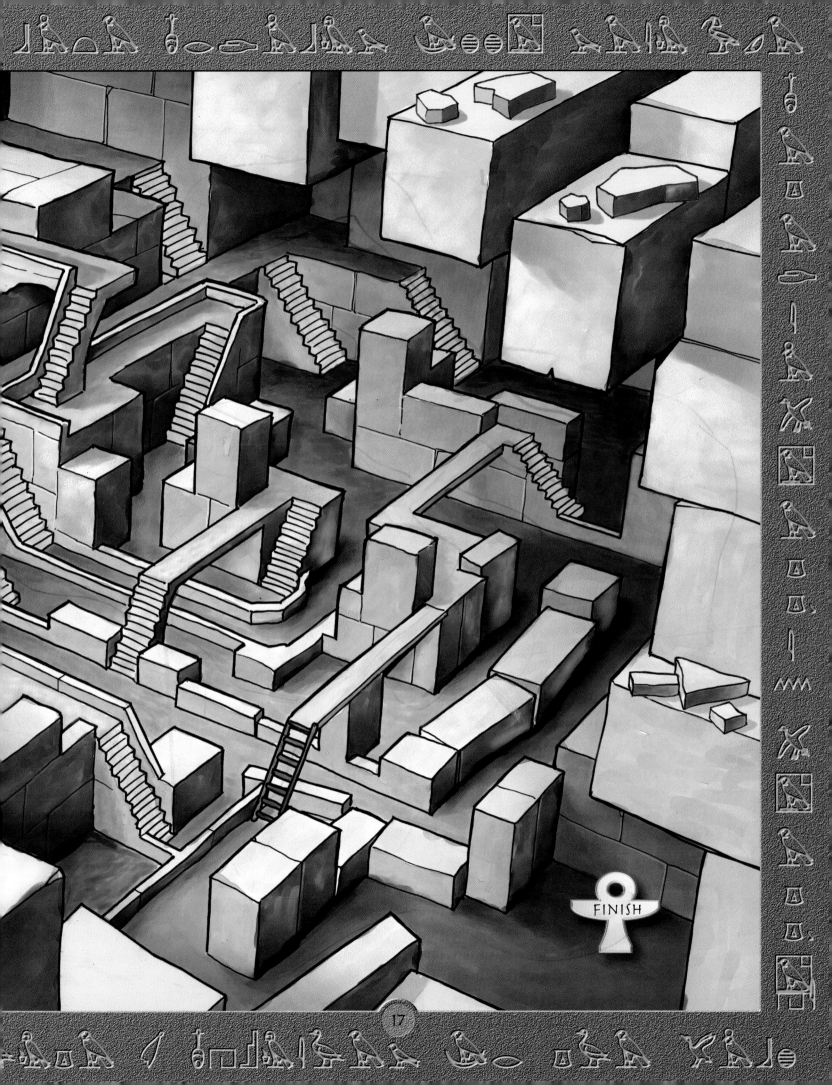

Say! This is starting to get interesting. The tunnel has led us to the very heart of the pyramid. We must be getting close to the Pharaoh's tomb. I thought I heard a sound! Could it be my father and his friends? If we can find our way through this chamber quickly, we might catch up with him.

Our writing, called "hieroglyphs," takes the form of small pictures or signs. Some represent just a letter, others a whole word. It takes many hours to write about our Pharaoh's life. We also write prayers and rituals to help our Pharaoh reach the next life. These are called "Pyramid Texts."

The Inner Chambers are full of wonderful paintings by our skilled artists. Some show gods helping our Pharaoh reach the next life and so are a bit like "living hieroglyphs." They look like hieroglyphs, too, because our artists draw what is in their own minds rather than represent what they actually see. But they paint on a square grid to ensure the proportions are correct.

Look! Some papyrus scrolls have been left here! Perhaps they tell of a way through the chambers. Sadly, poor families like ours can't afford proper schooling, and I cannot read. But I do know that the scrolls are made from strips of reed cut from the papyrus plant. The plant grows 13 feet high!

This scroll looks like a plan of the pyramid! Huge structures such as this need careful planning. This looks as if it could contain some of our architects' calculations.

The correct path leads to the Burial Chamber, where our Pharaoh's body is placed. I can hear voices echoing through the tunnels. I hope one is my father's!

So this is where our Pharaoh lies! He seems to be well provided for. But wait! I can just make out some figures on the other side of the chamber. It might be my father and his friends. We have to find our way to them.

The Pharaoh has been "embalmed." This process preserves his body for the afterlife. The body is first packed all around with special salt called "natron" for 40 days to dry out all the fluids. It is then washed and rubbed with oil and spices. The embalmers then carefully wrap the whole body in linen bandages and pour resin over it. The result is a "mummy."

When the mummy is completely finished, it is placed inside a wooden coffin beautifully carved and painted with bright colors. The priests then say prayers to ensure that the Pharaoh passes onto his next life unhindered. The chief embalmer, dressed as the god Anubis, blesses the body before it is placed inside an outer coffin of stone, called a "sarcophagus."

There are so many things buried with the Pharaoh! The possessions he used throughout his lifetime are for him to use in the afterlife. He will need furniture, tools, and clothes. We also often leave food, or stone models of food that we believe the Pharaoh can take the goodness from by using his powerful magic.

Statues of the gods are also left with the Pharaoh. When a pharaoh dies, we believe he becomes one with Osiris, the god of death and rebirth. Anubis, the jackal god, helps to judge the dead and also guards the tomb.

We must move quietly in case those people are not my father and his friends. If they are guards, we could be arrested as robbers!

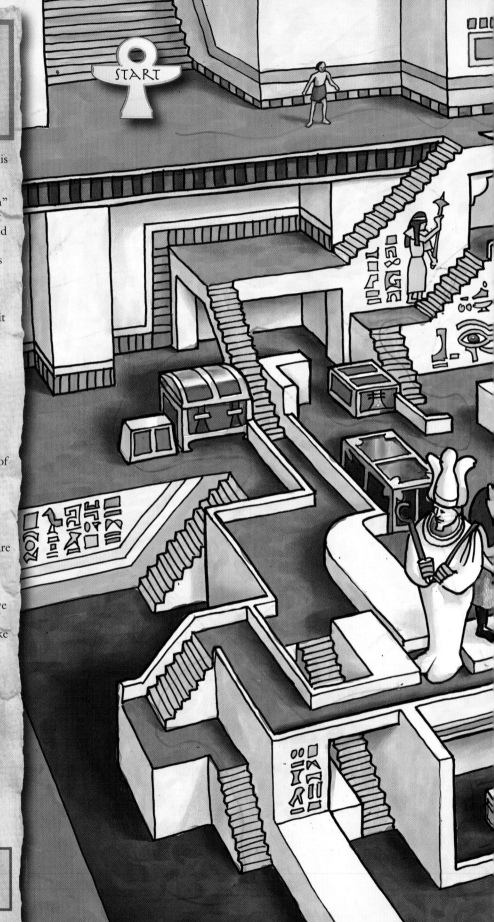

START

FINISH

Back with my father at last! But the entrance will have been sealed by now, and we are trapped. Father hopes there may be an escape tunnel if we can find it. But first we have to make our way to the Golden Shrine, in which my father has been ordered to place the "Canopic jars."

The Canopic jars hold the organs that have been removed from our Pharaoh. These organs have to be preserved so that the Pharaoh still has the use of his whole body in the afterlife. Each jar lid has a different head on it—a dog's for the stomach, a baboon's for the lungs, a human's for the liver, and a falcon's for the intestines.

Gold is plentiful in Egypt. Our craftsmen are very skilled at creating beautiful golden decorations for furniture, jewelry, and many other articles. Our gold can also buy us things that are scarce in Egypt, such as good timber. We import silver, copper, and ivory, too.

Magnificent jewelry is always buried with our pharaohs, such as pendants, rings, bracelets, and earrings, along with fans, statues, games, weapons, and elaborate model sailing boats. Even poor people are buried with some jewelry, in order to impress the gods when entering the afterlife.

The Golden Shrine is perhaps the most important treasure. It houses the Canopic chest, in which the jars are put. The chest is placed in the Shrine and sealed inside for eternity.

Father has found some hieroglyphs that tell of a secret tunnel leading to the valley temple near the Nile. But the tunnel door is shut tight. We have to work out how to open it. Turn the page and see if you can help us solve the secret code that will enable us to escape.

FINISH

CRACKING THE CODE

These are the hieroglyphs that my father discovered. They are written on a stone tablet next to the door of a secret tunnel that leads underground to the valley temple—and freedom. But it is locked, and before we can open it, we must crack the hieroglyphic code and fill in the white boxes on the stone with the correct letters. Some are already there, but we have to work out the rest to discover where the key that unlocks the door is hidden.

To show us which letters each symbol represents, the hieroglyphic key is written out on the left side of the stone.

Unfortunately, though, some of the hieroglyphs in the message are missing. To find them, you must first find each of the small drawings on the tablet, which are hidden somewhere in the pages of this book. When you find them, you will see that each one is pointing to the border of the page picking out the hieroglyph you need. Remember, we can't turn the page and make our escape until we have found where the key is hidden.

Good luck!

Symbol		Symbol	
= THAST		= REED	
= SEST		= ANTF	
= NTHE		= HELI	
= DOFT		= YISHI	
= PICJA		= HARA	
= LLGR		= DDEN	
= OHWI		= ERCI	
= HEKE		= CANO	
= THEM		= LCON	
= HEFA		= FULP	
= THOU		= OMWI	
= TDEAT		= HCUR	
= RTHA		= WITHI	

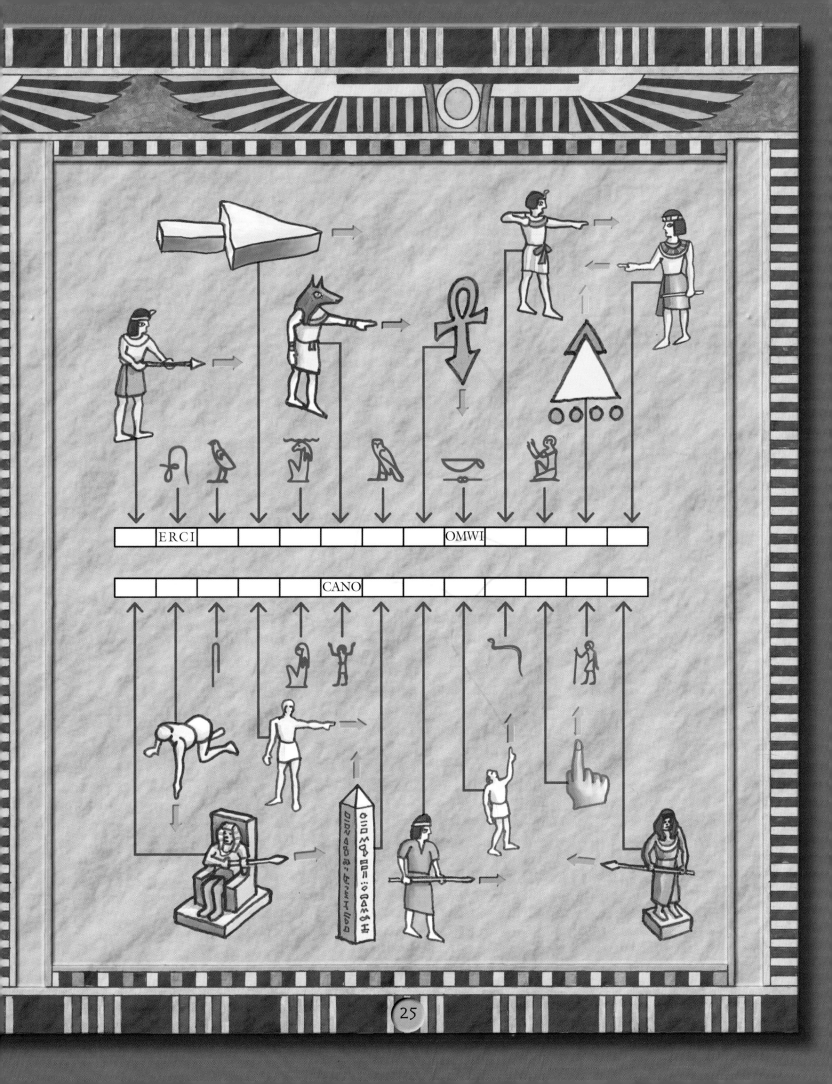

Well done! The code is cracked. Now all we have to do is find our way out through the secret tunnel. I long to see my mother again. She must be very worried about us. I can smell the fresh air from outside. It can't be too far now!

Our Pharaoh's body was received at the valley temple after his last journey down the Nile. Here, the funeral procession stopped and "the opening of the mouth" ritual was performed. This restores the Pharaoh's life powers, allowing him to eat, drink, and move. The mummy is lifted upright, and the mouth touched with instruments to symbolize the new life.

The procession, which continued to the mortuary temple near the pyramid, included the new Pharaoh, relations, high officials and priests,

and also professional mourners. These are hired to wail and to demonstrate the grief of all the people. They are very convincing!

We believe that to enter the afterlife, the Pharaoh will have to prove he is worthy by having his heart weighed against "the feather of truth." A

heavy heart indicates unworthiness and is fed to a monster. We believe that the body houses the "ka," which is the "life force" of a person. The body must be preserved for the ka to survive death and make an afterlife possible.

A false door to the pyramid is where food and sacred water are laid to keep the Pharaoh's ka alive. Statues of the Pharaoh are also washed and re-dressed to keep him clean and tidy in the afterlife.

At last, the end of our adventure is in sight! With a little more help from you to guide us out, we will be free at last. I'm so glad you joined me. I would never have found my father without you!

FINISH

START

SOLUTIONS

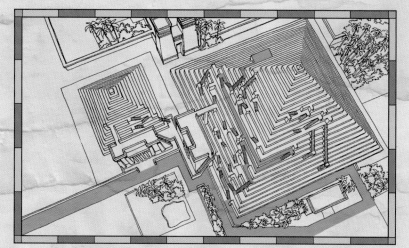

Maze 1. The Plan

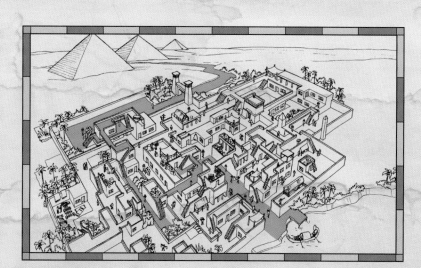

Maze 2. Off to the Pyramids

Maze 3. Construction Site

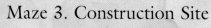

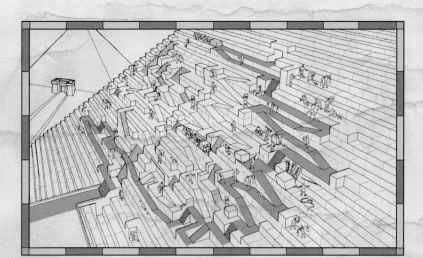

Maze 4. The Secret Entrance

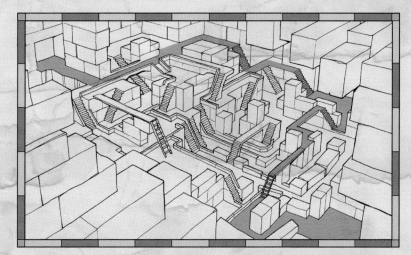

Maze 5. The Secret Tunnel

Maze 6. The Inner Chambers

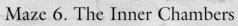

Maze 7. The Burial Chamber

Maze 8. The Treasure Chamber

The code cracked (use a mirror!)

The merciful Pharaoh will grant freedom without death curses.

The key is hidden in the Canopic jar that has the lid of the falcon.

Maze 9. Escape

Glossary

afterlife
To the ancient Egyptians, the afterlife was a bodily existence after death. At first, only pharaohs were entitled to an afterlife, but eventually all Egyptians could look forward to this life after death.

burial chamber
The strengthened room built at the center of the base of the pyramid to house the coffin.

Canopic jar
A jar with a lid in the form of a head, used to hold the organs removed from bodies before they are embalmed.

embalming
Drying out the fluids of a dead body, treating it with oil, and wrapping it to preserve it as a mummy.

feather of truth
A feather said to be used by the god Anubis to weigh against a dead person's heart to judge whether that person is worthy of an afterlife.

graffiti
Unofficial drawings or signs scratched or marked on stone.

granite
A very strong rock that can withstand great force without breaking.

hieroglyphs
The picture and sign writing used by the ancient Egyptians.

ka
The spirit of a person believed by the ancient Egyptians to live on after death if nourished. While the ka was kept alive, its owner would not die.

life force
The spirit said to exist in living things that is believed to guide their actions and thoughts throughout life.

limestone
A rock or stone used for building because it can be very easily carved without splitting.

mortuary temples
Temples, dedicated to the dead pharaoh, built close to the pyramids and where the pharaoh's body was brought to be mummified.

mummify
To preserve a dead body for burial.

mummy
An embalmed dead body, as prepared by the ancient Egyptians for burial and an afterlife.

overseer
A foreman in charge of a specific task or a group of workers.

papyrus
The writing paper made by the ancient Egyptians from the papyrus plant.

pharaoh
A king, or ruler, in ancient Egypt.

plumb level
A tool used to make sure surfaces are level.

professional mourners
People hired to demonstrate the grief of all of the people.

pyramid texts
Prayers and rituals designed to help the dead pharaoh reach his next life.

ramp
A temporary sloped surface used for transporting the stones up the pyramid.

right angle
A tool used to make sure that certain surfaces are perfectly upright.

sarcophagus
An outer coffin of stone, usually with carvings.

shrine
A place or container where relics of a dead person are kept.

soul
The part of a person that thinks and feels emotions, thought by many to exist separately from the body.

sphinx
A massive stone statue built by the ancient Egyptians. Most sphinxes had a human head and the body of a lion. Many were built to honor a pharaoh.

stonemason
A craftsman who worked and cut the great blocks of stone used in building the pyramids.

temple
The house of the gods, in which the ancient Egyptians worshiped and which also contained buildings for other activities.

valley temple
The temple on the banks of the River Nile where the funeral procession stopped for certain rituals before the pharaoh's body proceeded to the mortuary temple.

Index